I0185760

THE SIXTH GREAT EXTINCTION

THE SIXTH GREAT EXTINCTION

WHIT GRIFFIN

SKYSILL PRESS

Acknowledgements

Some of these poems have appeared in the following: *Cairn*; *Compost*; *Eccolinguistics*; *from a Compos't*; *H_NGM_N*; *Jellyroll*;*La Fovea*; *Leveler*; *Nejma*; *Sixth Finch*; *The Equalizer*; *The Montague Reporter*; *Turntable + Blue Light*; *Upstairs At Duroc*; *With + Stand*

Fugitive Cant originally appeared as *Empty Hands Broadside #18* (Country Valley Press)

Cathedral Ring originally appeared as a chaplet from Longhouse

"The Artificial Somnambulist" originally appeared as a broadside for The ___ Shaped Reading Series

Thanks also to my early readers

ISBN 978-1-907489-10-5

SKYSILL PRESS
3 Gervase Gardens
Clifton Village
Nottingham NG11 8LZ

skysillpress.blogspot.com

CONTENTS

I know these three
dimensions are but the top three and these five senses
only the first five.

—Guy Birchard, *from* 'Guy's Boast'

FOR THE OPENER OF LOCKS

OF BACON AND BROAD BEANS

If you can sit long enough
without killing or burning anything,
the forest will ease up and go
back about its business. I do
not advocate conserving the wilderness.
I advocate leaving the fuck alone.
The workaday world, somewhere
in the bluish distance, gives you
its brand of freedom. You can sing
a saucy farming song, or have your
teeth brought up to date. Forward-
thinking descendants of slaveholders
have revised the family history.
Now everyone operated a stop on
the underground railroad. Grackles
amid the strawberries. Grandma
died on the morphine and there was
a fight over her box fan. Ask Thomas
Bewick how he got a swan named after
him. Finally, validation of my idea
for a chandelier of bread. I knew that
sinfonietta would change your tune.

BOAR HUNTING IN THE ZONE OF ALIENATION

In order to form a more
utopian society I'll have to
ask two-thirds of you to leave.
The only hope is that we
eradicate ourselves quickly, that
the species that take over from
us can exist in our fumes. From
George Starkey to Thomas Midgley
Jr, have the alchemist's progeny
enhanced our plight at all? On
friendly terms with the unseen
world, the intrepid goat wrinkling
past. Hold your own light on
the next plateau of understanding. The
mighty ridge of Iapetus. Half
the year spent in the sacred mountain,
half dancing for hot rain. We must
repeal the mining law of 1872. If
only we could have hare with our
pappardelle. *Wisdom is what you get*
when you don't get what you want.
Where is the life-bringer, the full
basket? Made blood brothers by
the bed bug. You've turned your
hand to many things. Your shaman
wields a scalpel.

SCARAB, SAIL AND BUCKLE

Come through winter only to face
the darkest months. The bodies
of the drowned were never buried
in the churchyard proper, but on
the outskirts, lest the sea wanted
to reclaim them. *We are spiritual*
beings having a human experience.
To have a friend out in the fog, in
the middle of the weather. The best
place for watching rough ocean's inside
a lighthouse. *There were five hundred*
and eighty doors in Valhalla, and eight
hundred warriors poured from each
door. Easier to imagine the carnal
weapons of Elagabalus; suffocating
the less fortunate under rose petals.
Pity the majority of believers who
only embrace one god. The panther's
fragrant breath allures a multitude.
The capstan can weigh great anchors,
but it too has a threshold for strain.

THE SAINTLY THIEF

Faster than the panthers in sun
and rain. I have created my own
rites of passage, a new way
of proposing execution. Lenin
promised the people pisspots
of gold. Don't seize the theatre,
take the police station. It's
the revolt, not the murder, which
is beautiful. Can you separate
revolution from violence? Violence
in the chanting; the poem from
the ritual? The feeling could only
be expressed in the form chosen. *I
can be at ease now, I know I will go
from one miracle to the next.* Your
questions are good, but I can't
tell the whole truth.

ELEVEN ON THE OTHER SIDE

The ancients performed dissections
on living criminals. For stealing
bread you'll further our understanding
of the stomach. Fed on scraps
in an effort to stave off a hunger
in the mind. An image with
no attribution, the historian's con-
undrum. The residue of an active
imagination. An insignia sewn
to be stripped off in humiliation.
Blindfolded when the epiphany came,
a tempest of sparrows singing in
their sleep. To attach the wild
bird's song onto a manmade staff.
Their innocence in a sense tipping
into mockery. Puzzled by the
complexity, a whole new scale
is needed. Like a comet
made new with each visitation,
its train luminous, its orbit undefined.

GREGARIOUS FLOWERING

Think you're uptown with those pre-
cut screens. Secure in your own co-
herence. Do you dance or have a dowry?
Call it camouflage but I say they're
dressed in the materials of their surroundings.
The mandibles remain visible. Distributing
a clean death to the unwashed masses.
The rain doesn't need rescuing. The waltz
finally loses its innocence. *Ample color*
and vivacity in the swirl of enigmatic events.
Dirge-like throbbing betrays no terror. You
can be like St. Anthony of Padua and preach
to the fishes. I'll heat up the oil.

ALTERED COURSES

Fat in the fall of a mast year,
wary of the mice that will follow.
You don't want to leave too much
to the imagination. The bigger
the moon the smaller the candle.
Every life-affirming action contains
a thousand invisible annihilations.
Who on this planet doesn't know
the shape of a gun? Is it a
comfort to think the other animals
don't know they face extinction?
There'll be fewer to name in the
language that replaces this one.
Watch the slow motion reshuffle.
When a buckaroo gets that leaving
look every mustache and veil turns
moist. A pity there's been a
fudge in nature's allegory. Put fish
on that spinach. Point out the
verdant hillside where sheep may
safely graze. So this is how
the stalwarts meet their end.
Caught between the consequence
and the punishment.

EVERY MAN ALONE

There are those who set out
on a path that will lead to their
judging of others. There are those
who assassinate heads of state and
those who shun the cocktail party.
Acts which active men must perform.
The act is always awkward if
performed in hiding. No decisions,
but certain facts. I'll give you
rent-free space in my head, but
you must hand over your evolutionary
destiny. Instinct leads me back
toward my own. I assert that any
man can valorize any word. I listen
in the dark to a language that goes
unformulated.

JUNGLE TELEGRAPH

The frustration of a man with vision
but no vocabulary with which to convey it.
An expensive bandage, a deity sooty
in the mind. Limited but not un-
mistakable, companion to foxes. Riding
out a storm in a cyclone-prone part
of the world, picturing all the helium
sequestered beneath the Great Plains.
Prior to porcelain, anterior teeth were
harvested from corpses. At one time it
was supposed *oysters came to the surface*
at night and opened their shells, into which
fell dewdrops that turned into pearls. Plan
to improvise. I'd prefer to be back at the fabulous
paradise I was stationed at before. Tang of heather,
comfort of barley. A pro on the malt plow.
Stuck in a damp cell with a less than absorbent mop.

COYOTE BLUES

I went from doubting the existence
of my own spirit to believing everything
has a soul. The sacred stories
can only be told on winter nights, when
the animals can't hear us talking
about them. The holy idiom
of moonshining deacons. Your task
for tonight is to learn the names of
two thousand roses. Wode thistle
sounds nicer than poison parsley. We're
cursed to die, and feel sorry
for each other. Take your inner voice
into account. Whales are committing
suicide because of sonar. We're
being guided by blind men who insist
they can see.

KICKING DOWN AN OPEN DOOR

Hold my mule while I shout.
My church is the corner of the
courtyard. This country's like
a syphilitic, proud of his huge
cock. If you've never seen an
eagle you may think the hooked
beak is a fighting injury. Don't
let yesterday take up too much
of today. Revolution smells
like rotting produce. I'd like
to write the biography of each
mountain martyred for coal. After
we trek across the mountains,
gliko. Sluggish after birthday
cake. A late polish. Taught to
stay tight. *Touch that string most*
which makes best musick.

THE GLEANERS

The light cannot be too bright.
Uncertain instruction if ignorant
of the inflection. *It appears horrible*
to chew and swallow the flesh of
an animal which holds its young
to its breast, which is formed exactly
like that of a woman, with paws
resembling human hands. Like the
manatee, mythical mermaid of the sea,
we too are set to be slaughtered. It's
easier to live lavishly than consciously.
Accommodate chance and turn off the push.
Not all ground is apt for generation.
Bury the ears broken off a stone
statue under the outhouse door
to know what names the baron calls
his mistress. He knows how to work
the machine if the machine is working,
but not how to fix the machine if the
machine is broken.

BENIGN VIOLATION

Breakfast nervous with a threatening
fandango. Did your egg not set
this morning? Can't roast a dill pickle
before it turns black. Gratuitous
yet beautiful. Never on the wrong
side of the mountain. Enough blue
sky to cover a Dutchman's britches.
Let's revel in our sentience as we stroke
our incunabula. What comes first,
the form or the name of the form?
Where is that tree with which I shared
such affinity? The hostile apologist
negates his own philosophy.
Displacement by fire or flood, who's
to say what constitutes the world's
end? Let each individual determine
their own apocalypse. Each flower
contains the means of its own
regeneration. The divine automaton
constructs its own creation myth.
Cursed with retention but not recall,
making do without remittances. At
home in a nation ruled by Ares.

XENON THE STRANGER

Swifts through the waterfall, curator of meteorites.
She is beautifully-shod, the waker of those who
sleep. Great Mother, who sent Christ to rescue
Sophia. Splendor of morning, monocle of the Great
Eye, E over Delphi. The dawn chorus broadcasts
its story of another night's survival. To live in colder
climes, where suicide is as simple as staying outside.
Not unpleasantly ferocious, this desire to evacuate.
The illusion and hope that in death all will be revealed,
resolved. Hard to love someone who doesn't think
you make the cut for inclusion in their afterlife. Glory
in metaphor, reject theology. Adapting on the edge
of reason, from zenith to collapse. That some day no
winged thing will have ever seen one of our kind.

POOR MAN'S PARASOL

It's doubtful he was ever here
and you're holding your breath
for him to come back. How long
has bacon been a vegetable? Your
job is to flower where planted, not
pine over where you wish you were.
I can pay you in azalea blossoms
come springtime. Leave it to our
leaders to turn peonies into poison.
All we can ask for is a little sunlight
at our times of dying. Now I'm
suspended in the heavens, showing
off my acroamatics, nostalgic for
the Forest of Arden. The tree with
copper bark. My titanium armadillo.

THE NEW ENUMA ELISH

Whoever said we had dominion
over the earth had shit for
brains. Get that tattooed on
your forearm. It's one thing
to reject a notion, something
else to propose a new conception.
To proffer a radical vision.
Once a flamingo finds a mate
it lets its feathers fade. *It's*
almost like a ferret becoming an
otter. Accomplished on the bull-
roarer. I missed you when you
were underground. *When I came*
to my senses I was covered in blood,
and I was in a canal. As the
Alpine mischiefmaker hands out
birch switches, don't put all your
assets next to the sea. They
ate bandicoots until there were none.
They came to honor me with turnip
greens and I smiled, happy.

OLD SINS LONG SHADOWS

The sun is not a light
bulb, it's a hydrogen bomb.
The moon moves the tides,
not the dogma of desert fathers.
The Tiber is no longer muddied
with the ashes of cremated owls.
Those who claim immortality
is within reach have underestimated
the negative effect oxygen has
on our bodies. Look at the
fortune to be made convincing
people the way they live is normal.
Savor the sorrow to come
with the vivid kick. Old
people will mumble about flying
machines that used to convey meat
animals and fruit from across the
great waters, and will be cursed as
liars by those born in the post-
petroleum age. Linger lovingly on
the dance. Grade it a pleasure to
have lived before scholarship took
a backseat to survival. To have
probed the thinnest air for the
whole thought. It's nice to imagine
our protector chooses to be beautiful.

SUMMERLAND

Petrified and despotic the economist
and theologian both fix prices on the
diadem comfortably sucking the slender
vegetation amazed with the wave's
harmonious power hip of the wild rose
tender mark made in a ritual of mutual
abuse friendly in their shrinking minds
a famous love letter containing a recipe
calling for damson juice

•

Dizzy on the mat casting
a tanned hand to some underground
freedom based on written proof a
sincere servant found staggering
among the purslane a woven
basket in the fat public snow
embarrassed at the reunion by
the mouse-colored horse jumpy
around the landmine from a
family that won't abide cold meat
take a long and easy breath a royal
flame heats a happy bathtub

The spinning mill's become unraveled
addicted to the primary primitive
the smile based on jailbird obscurity
he's not to be relied on rejoicing
silkworm bricklayer permission to
track the boy scout back to his hovel
yellow raspberry tamarisk makes
the camel kneel led astray following
the wrong pervert honor chastity
pander to the cuckold buried treasure
under the brothel a cynic won't
buy an unripe melon it's either
a butterfly or a raft made of inflated
sheepskins

•

Rising of a star appearance
of a tooth a birth a rowdy
member of a disbanded fire
brigade wearing a crest of
horsehair the railway sleeper
makes suspicious improvisations
spongy lady torpedo the
tortoise the young bull a
kind of lark inexperienced
with charcoal on a worldly
minded wavelength

Counted among the clamoring delirious
the chase finished villa canopied
and estimable to walk with
a quivering gate aggressive in
satin check the cistern for
garlic and generosity a journey
is just an earnest voyage flightily
laden with rue pertaining to
the early dawn the poor ambassador
shed blood in a drunken death struggle
hopscotch at the public fountain
a musical instrument made out of carp

•

Deduction and aptitude to hold
a Spanish bantam a stalactite
is as useful as a billiard cue to
a lobster a mackerel in a frock
coat scurvy mariner in the
sportsman hospital a pair of
silent slippers hit the mark
in high elevation powerfully built
but impotent plan on being festive
despite fortifications the
concubine found an electric squirrel
small steamboat in a stagnant pond
a written petition a jealous prayer for rain

Go raiding very quickly and find
a remedy for crust around the eye
silence the blabber carry official
correspondence to the jangler
in the belfry a fish hook with
several points a pine kernel
agitated by industrious cobblers
rowing hard in the saddle a
castanet seizure cream cheese
kite above the steam hammer shop

•

Pluck the hairless clover wild
unbroken trefoil act of chipping
stone dispatch highwaymen shameless
gaping sheiks of fear render
non-existent quilt-needling plague-
stricken wash-house patriots tangerine-
turbaned Jonah turtle dove swallowed
in the calm open sea high loud voice
a lisping jest trousers made of wax
paper a fine horseman a large pearl

All at once the bay tree went
bald an obstinate maternal
uncle lean and rely on the bass
drum creditor the register of landed
property rather narrow in his
nostalgic insomnia his plaintiff
earthenware hydrophobia Darwinism
in the school for orphans in utter
confusion the dance became peppery

•

Inciting compassionate anatomy disgusting
fossil jeering and colonized intoxicants
collected for the paralyzed sultan a military
band their instruments carried by pack
animals puff ball asparagus short-sighted
prosperity to gird oneself with sacred ketchup
blank shot in dry society recover one's losses
escape through the worm hole like a rodent
to the very marrow noble and clammy as it
used to be automatic and inoffensive in ecstasy

Imprisoned in the okra burnt
confidence choked engraver
true nature of the thing a
prohibited orbit gold coins
and protégés vacant and dethroned
condemned creatures with bashful
surnames vulgar sadness beaten
with a wing sweet dish of
supernatural mineral water heavy
feverish scimitar a miserable rag

•

German silver whiskers heaven-scented
useless vanity intelligent weather-prophet
the opening splashing noise dividing
lewd wind-bag harlots glorious in
immoral deeds a wife with a colorful
thigh profit from a whispering evil
intent flick the fingers in the cartridge
factory a philosopher on a small buoy
a flotilla of ivory garden mallets think
on the elephant bishop so and so Good
God Alive sweet basil fillet

Civilized and falsely claiming to be
retired a specialist moved by
the oppressor's dashing axiom symmetrical
mint vizier dervish annulment tender
church bell a thin tune rarely
occurring knocked out in cash unknown
germinating regret unheard of white
heat trumpeter ventilating mass
exquisite impurity coquettish unclean
blessed boon-companion

•

Lying superficially bare slippery
flame messenger a vegetable stuffed
with rubies nearing the willow
a certain wakefulness grips the
enemy butter plunders the rain
glitter orgy shining gorgeous held
responsible tonguing falsehood lacquered
barefoot and lumpy the fall of the leaf
sticky in the ear sneak off
and make a lop-sided volcano

lame thick round oar beetle
the large artilleryman cripple
the covetous plump gold-plated
caterpillar pretend not to shiver
having wheels a bubbling hookah
an oblong melon a deep helmet
twine angel ghost of the milky
dream sawdust calendar a damp
Russian peasant signs establishing
monastic orthodoxy taker of
bribes on the windward side face
to face with firmness a demolished plough

•

Tropical prison a drunkard in ruins
tax the great families zodiac larynx
ladybird honeysuckle warbling at the
stud farm home-destroying affair
chat with stingy piety green as
fodder in summer shorts motionless
earthquake sack made of haircloth
bastard scoundrel running irascible

Intolerant onionskin old fashioned
fanatic devotee of dining table
mystics punctilious garden seller
frigid pickle sodium hyena glaze
the mystery in a smell of recognition
given to grinning at the butler in leather
thong direct road of ill-timed fortune
we who share a common ear-hole

•

Balance the minister so that licensed
prostitutes make a present of varnished
blood vessels gulp down food in
accordance with the astute hypotenuse
utter abuse in his presence spacious
keepsake desert importance a squawking
visa purple without a middle
clearness to be in love with thunder
notorious ointment you are in luck
halfway between juiciness and a raceway peninsula

Growing old is optional a violent examination
a singer's chant identifies their home
village cruel mouthpiece falling down
English style keep others at one's
expense eclipse the manifestation
metaphor for loan faulty semolina
skeleton bidder reactionary liaison
who does his work hinders tripe wrinkle
down safety razor Japan

•

Disgraceful in his bushy beard
knuckle down show off the buttocks
at dawn throw dice crazier
in a lattice cage all-powerful
cuttle-fish cardiac heart rattle
dazzle the teeth lunar whiplash
spirit lamp hunchback calcium galoshes

Lick oneself in a sparkling manner kingfisher
lightning a lie has a short life fawning
medieval youthful horse-blanket sham
tundra well-fleeced wool merchant
great owl pickpocket of mature years squat
batter soaked in syrup in the act of being
spread out for publication

•

Rising without due course roadless
and unmannerly banned by his guild
despoiled in a slow motorcar good
luck vitriol brazen-faced trembling
mammal this doctor recognizes
rheumatism at the corner deli garfish
horoscope harmless olive eccentric bridegroom

Sneeze-provoking evening of nautical
salutes capsized haberdasher daubed
with incongruous colors spend the
whole day feeling beat down plaster
of Paris ordinary troop speculation
deceived by showy organs vague
redness formerly a flourishing
surgical process a legendary bird

•

Ice factory suckling calf covered
bent double presumptuous nostril
cross-word tower celestial steed
smeared contagious thick soup whirling
intestine utterly bored gadfly
sorcery humbly swaggering worthless
lozenge high stakes double-breasted
spiteful old hag we shook hands

Chatterbox eternal passionate monster
lover of money space vault of heaven
powder ammunition newspaper beggar
atavistic cunning beauty flowing
dagger of darling rock tweezers
seller of livers world conqueror
tyrannical mosquito net funeral shrew

•

Brave alcoholic immensely wealthy German
fern root let no one think this refers
to him Neapolitan meddler blind invalid
standard bearer accustomed to tame tactful
bracelets six-shooter wedding ring electrical
intercourse empirical pitiless granary with
full details pineapple maternity now the
matter is clear The Ruddy Goose

Extremely white oak tree daughter of Eve
eternal sea port dug with a spade fasten
mankind stupidly to one's tongue committed
to memory celibate watchman without a share
leopard moonlight castle of Bedouin waste
A great work of art oblivious and malevolent be
mine narcotic drug resembling epidermis

•

Head knob hemorrhoids too late
heavy sundial the sense of sight
Prime Minister ancient war-galley
honeycomb paper if I could only get
news of him pillow vagabond fraudulent
borrower pig-headed spit of land glib
person pustule sewing workshop

Polished copper summersault skull-cap
cutwater palpitation sterile stationary
soft words squeezing a small loaf
typhoon band spectral mutation greyhound
cyclamen refrigeration allegiance daring
reprimand lazy prince pleasure resort
Russian meat-safe boasting bitter telegraph

•

Mumble chew rhinoceros horn
stretched taut weather large truly
sewer shrub ship youthful dropsy
weasel poppy jagged iron rake
nuptial chamber notch in an arrow
creaky membrane confused traveler
nasal song twang hidden garment
nutritious tickling pocket knife

Wish God-speed brusquely at heart he's
a coward present arms soundless octogenarian
generosity of sovereign vituperative Great
Wall of China flat wicker basket ephemeral
lard melancholy passenger looseness of
texture worthy of his father's damp protection

•

Prosperous water yellow writing paper
wearing a poor mandrake strange
ebony climate incoherent blockade
waifs and strays promptly exchange
sharp illusions horse radish a
kind of cucumber implement for opening
appetizers without fulfillment wide
awake cunning chap garden sage
rabbit without servants sweetheart citron

Semi-solid unwholesome jewel
become heavier with hospitality
gaping obscene cotton address
book opium excommunication
raspberry woodpecker halo poison
good to eat mouthpiece lachrymose
oneness cicada axe the common
people buying majestic judgment

•

Fine drizzle sigh Red Sea wild pear
spooky octopus squinting spittle
birth tree eunuch wisdom tooth I
want nobody's interference on the contrary
clever advisor village elder limping
vermillion dynasty alfalfa joker
perpetual fever hollow kidney bean

Scorch the connection December retreat
alphabet chill a present the return
of which is demanded six goldsmiths
useless but harmless topsy-turvy
intentional cousin soiled with love
safe capable of journalism marsh
mellow midwifery literate unbound
pharmacy will-o-the-wisp mummy

•

Legs astraddle forks evident latrine
crisis night patrol casual Argentina
porter's saddle minimum rebel acid
expression newly married mother of pearl
light the fuse fire-worshipper panic
at the sardine factory small churn

Chandelier second childhood you'll get
nothing skirmishers glow-worm turkey
on this very spot buttermilk nitrogen
molar tooth saintly practical old man
henceforth the sublime almond rope
of duck zephyr swaddling aubergine
Balkan hunchback aphrodisiac whalebone

•

Erotic acrobat botanical bovine
Arctic spice hoodwink hemlock
dealer in honeymoons smeared with
dapple-gray high-flying saboteurs
manna drinking mug manifest barium
ear of corn overcome giddiness without
a head for sinking toy veterinarian

Resurrection dysentery who sees stamped
copper squat sweetmeat what can't be
cured as stiff as a poker simplify
pain sloppy sheepdog gambling den
abusive owl darling brawler a
bird of prey helpless and invisible
sultan's mother holding festive battery

•

A day of mourning fools some of them
abrogated erroneous by virtue
backbiter ether objective spirits varicose
veins cherishing a grudge magnanimous manifesto
five yard starfish a similar face hired
horses capable of thinking pimento rosary
tubby louse bottle divorce wheat steam
green glass circus The Angel of Death

Dossier feast turn blind on all fours
curse anyone up and down high class
disheveled womb foundry stuffed
gallop bushy eyebrows smoke lip
mulberry garden wrought iron lament
consummate parrot tender groove barge

•

Pathetic sensation limpid heifer
yesterday's tobacco decay Aegean
diversion well-behaved inner rib
lamentation expert vigorous cultivator
chief coffee-grinder in short pipe tube
carnivorous purple bear bowels fresh
vermicelli five bushels hashish vowel

Having moles on the ears venerable
ball-bearing white-wash sandal
quarter circumference unhusked rice
meat threaded on a stick top of
secular mermaid crawfish anchor
altruistic cerebellum kneecap jelly
Billy-goat private captive kitten gravy

•

Take it back squash injury
furrow eternal book of samples
equine greatness superhuman prune
petticoat watermark slip-knot silly
catch a fish in someone's bootstrap
sudden gush syringe loin-cloth

Flying nutcracker an absence of jurisprudence
leaping in a whisper yellow branches lukewarm
obtuseness gargling westward fury cause
to be late evening primrose linseed delphinium
inverted itching comma natural strangle water
lily breeding buried azure bib crow behind
magic fallow deer rose-water sun-fish chamomile

•

Good morning ghost pigeon bombast
in autumn wickedness crucify quite
fresh fritter reunion tasty slaughter-house
set a trap causing inner constraint trifle
dwelling recluse secret rabbi paternal
aunt genuine folklore clumsy pavilion
feigning votive mutton pederast enthronement

Hot prison granny half-baked extortion
pious deeds backgammon shriveled politician
exposure uneducated perfume candle power
pleasant little wench creeping insect calligraphy
remember gratis airman top-heavy barking
like a lion artificial worry geometrical tumult

•

Every ubiquitous decrepit herd neighboring
digestive camel corps snail shell propeller
stingy busybody calculating bunches of grapes
hung up to awake the desires chicory satire
crafty nutmeg castor-oil cock hammer hare-brained
schoolmaster coy cereal boundary overlooked
syrup hang-over bloodthirsty hermaphrodite needle

Give without stint accept favorable silk thread
idiot son evident eruption invent secondary school
capital punishment maintain social mineral administration
incorrigible twisted pin-prick break a fast
intermixture afternoon prayer advertisement elixir
to exalt as a syphilis spring slope explosion

•

Trust monopoly infectious cupbearer
will-power groan cessation policeman
horseshoe timber divination by dreams
a kind of sea-bream Swedish news
service bring to fruition a show of hands
corroded rainbow fear of nightshade

Small hatchet dark and dirty lime-tree
sob cavalry charge put forth catastrophe
heat rash hideous technical spinach
verbose bone bandit spasm cabinet
coasting nightmare ladylike fugitive

•

Unlucky land survey country of infidels
cellulose rhyme crack overpowering Cairo
oracle prostitution coffee tray polecat
hip hose cardamom pavement goal-keeper
whipping carpet calico gizzard illicit
buckwheat vampire assassin cheese

Scratching the back tambourine welding
two sides of the rump boilermaker partridge
heinous sin tartar on the teeth shroud
goose cabbage guttersnipe chestnut monk

•

Drawn discoveries beggar's bowl great
confusion Mt. Olympus diploma flax
librarian eyelash massacre of gentle birth
renal cumin guillotine The Crimea
very short pincers writhe elegant minced
unmarried cuff-link eat maize violently

Other people's whims winding gold
tavern flatter timid bucket chorus
scarecrow collar-bone blind at random
leather watch-chain ear-flap turret
frog tumor dovetail hairdresser hempseed
extreme bird's-eye saucepan piano comet
turned to ashes foul-mouthed mimosa

•

Lapis-lazuli let go wishbone
alluvial soil nonchalant rice pudding
picking figs pancake dialect lemonade
lilac stork signboard chamber pot lynching
holding ether fickle sugar Sodomite metaphysics
goat's milk Meerschaum cloudiness choked
combustible scissors magnolia windsail

Stratagem squid lettuce gone before beating
dismissed official driven away loop-hole cudgel
powerless watercolor small crescent possible
diabolical angel leper promenade marble
place of arrival test-tube cabin-boy

•

Things arrived suitable for liquorice root
blind mile axis verbena pulpit elbow
shilly-shallying short-sighted enigma
hump-backed emigration Zoroastrian stockbroker
tormented contemporary motor encyclopedia
sacred mucous shaking stone wardrobe

Arrogant sideboard worrying coffin
who waits in an orderly manner blow
with the fist proof-reader fragrant parenthesis
face to face copulation refrigerator expressed
banana autocracy composed painful gentleness
astrologer laxative docile governess suicide
spendthrift hard to please on lease dropsical

•

Oblong reservist carrying level mustard
organic retrograde haughty hoping oozing
out hybrid creatures incognito parallelogram
gilded chronicler thronging carpenters
quash asthma written to resemble a
prohibition gorilla pertaining to sleep

Countless marriage half marksman
the choicest part Norway carouse
January furnace ejaculate cricket omelet
backbone middle-class bull grotto dupe
thirty short-lived nectarine diaper
urinal oppression knitted cobwebs anvil
trouser leg paraffin Parmesan thrashing

•

All of a sudden a whacking decoy potato
footsteps rowdy cracker vice-admiral
plumb-line abstinence flatter freshwater
pear-shaped gem being cooked immature
vain hope shabby leek platinum idol

Puff pastry camel spot quiet tassel
who bribes reading-desk pendulum
vernal raisin hospital inspector suffrage
fennel cursive jigger bowing majority ship
suavity prosperity pure butter beast
kept for white blaze dare-devil

•

House on the sea-shore ownerless
without milking rubbish paralyzed
slug listeners sarcophagus epileptic fit
fir-cone stomach-ache sarsaparilla wasp
check pattern summer swift-footed
eight Friday arrows ricochet little
fingers fruitful fat millstone pretext

Cypress diabetes lightning-conductor
cigarette case dervish's cap vinegar
insurance box on the ear without a rag
dental age marigold urgency secret grin
somewhat friendly oval hardness hang
sausage sesame bayonet otter along

•

Languid testimonial to play the iris
peregrine scarf smacking cemetery peach
ardent desire Bosporus ferry steamer
jock martyrs stink slipper pistol levity
submarine sea-saw be all square
night-cap tango fez comb certified virility
collect the works of pavement gladden
all by himself haunted mullet filigree
tincture of seal generation metempsychosis
warning radish ornamental knob sweat

FUGITIVE CANT

ELEGANT HICCUP

How interested are you in knowing
what's going on? How what was known
as truth changed with the advent of
writing. There's always room for rumor
in what passes as the new normal.
Whose hidden friend left the wicker
cornucopia and expired phone directory?
A book of that size would fell an ox.
Much is made of the pantomime villain's
secret gestures. Her dancing gives her
circulation. Sally Rand can't fan dance
her way into the falconer's arms. Falcons
won't breed when lemmings are scarce.
It's unlucky to eat horse meat before
mounting a chariot. There's a big
difference between food that won't make
you sick and food that's good for you.
Ring the dinner bell, it's time we taste
the *wulf*. The first thought of many
is to fear the foreign, and to kill it.
Some people's eyes are better at seeing
tomorrow. Ask the teahead in the corner.
Let's get out of here, he's starting
to resolve. The river runs south to north,
not that that impresses the fish.

THESEUS AND THE MINOTAUR

A feast with flagons.
The wrong wedding
guest is offered wine and the bride
turns up missing.
I'm sorry.
I thought you said *pièce de résistance*,
not *fiesta*.
To mingle in generation. Autonomous
as a bronze bell, clapper
long abandoned. Long time spent
watching horses
wade streams.
Do you have a magic
ball of thread? Is that a getting up or a bearing down
grip? The speech
inside the stone is the source of your complaint.

DAY RUN THROUGH WITH TIME

Anvils and oboes announce autumn's
departure. *Profundity and a sense of*
celebration. The last cup of hot
chocolate before the seasons change.
Bar Betty from the door, but let
our merriment be. The lobelia's been
planted; now we wait on the pollinators.
We've come through a winter where
we began to wonder if it ever really was
warm. A quick hit from the coping wand
will work wonders. Use the violin
as a compass. How can a fish taste
of the stable? We have an area devoted
to breeding rabbits. Keep the strawberries high.

PULLED FROM THE QUIRE

Don't waste your money on wicker
baskets. Eels find peas irresistible.
Just wait for them to swim into
your field. All day there are those
who wish us to believe they belong
above us. Don't think the tide
turning in your favor will turn their
attitude toward you. It takes
a lifetime to overcome the sensitivity.
Mirth, the quick takeaway. Look
for the grace in each fleeting gesture.
If I could only have seen a hummingbird
fly, it would have been an epoch
in my life. The mountaineers do not
huddle, ageless endurance of the
elderly. Leggy and delicate, the foxes
frisk and gambol on ancestral ground.
Each day carries its own color.

RAGS THE DIGGER

How did we come to know
where all these roads lead
if we did not build them
ourselves? There's been a melee
in the middle, but violence
does not affect our bond. Since
we're blood I'll kick you
with my weaker foot. This is
a good time to leap, no matter
your height. There are plenty
of nasty people, but no evil trees.
A robin is not a redstart. A scold
of jays has made their presence
known, but the wrens will have
vengeance in the end. The
scent is so strong from the overgrown
butterfly bush the hummingbirds forego
the manmade feeder. No one has to
tell the other animals what to eat.
Prune the fig tree. If you plant
the rapeseed I'll have cups struck
to commemorate the harvest. Breadfruit
kept Captain Bligh on Tahiti. No
sign of mutiny in this handsome orange,
this rainbow trout. You'll never catch
a big fish in these waters again.

PERFECT ENOUGH

Cowper's leech foretold thunder.
A beautiful way to reject the surprise
that lurks in darker parts.

Dressed modestly but wielding
a hammer, when he hits his groove
you know where the sound comes from.

In your case I'd say it's safer to know
for certain the few plants that can kill
you instead of trying to keep up with
the myriad that will do you well.

I practice an everyday animism, of the
walking around variety. The awareness
that everything is imbued with divinity.

This is for our brothers on the other side,
who can't tell the difference between a barn
swallow and a bluebird.

The coin I carry says, To Thine Own Self Be True.

TREATING THE CRIPPLER

ALL THE WAY TO BUTTERNUT

Burning bald to general revel. Five logs
make a good fire. A bad man will turn
his face from an open flame. Coffee
grounds clean a chimney. Shown a spider
pipe, I'm still hooked on the calabash. The
cat with the cancerous paw attacks the wheatgrass.
Not just faithful to the early visions, the tiles
tell a story of revelation. Halfway through
the afternoon the ring gets cursed. Oyster
shells around the fig tree. A beach of jasper.
Blooming amaryllis and a jade egg. We couldn't
find mussels in Jonesport so we drove on
to Machias. This is grandfather clock for beginners.
You can't eat it but it feeds. At least you can
recognize a grapefruit spoon. I know what looks
good on your face. If Mozart didn't exist we'd have
to invent him. Turkeys laid eggs on the outhouse
roof, so we made omelets.

SHANGO OWNS THE DRUM

There's nothing I can do
to make this tuber mature
faster. Bring the ground
truth to the naked ear. Earth
in the square, the lucent center.
The fight between lumpers &
splitters, the raft & the riverside.
Finn's wisdom came from the salmon
he ate, not the thumb he sucked. I
can't just move to the Kalahari &
start running. These revelations
open onto their own journeys. Ask
the man who's planted twenty thousand
trees, the knots burn hottest.

GREEK OWL BLUE, NEW PENNY GREEN

I know a man who refuses to help
the poor for fear their plight will
inhibit his progress. Suicide is
the enemy of the moneylender.
These mountains will remain
majestic long after the coins in
your pocket have ceased to carry
currency. How many gods have
grown extinct in the presence of
these stones? One more war and
we'll be back to writing on clay.
Fire is the great purifier. *Let*
the curiosity to know the future be
silenced forever. Have you been
to Baalbek? Can we say the Aztec
were wrong in believing chaos
would envelope the world if the
sun weren't fed human blood?
Pharaoh's perfume has evaporated.
Our bountiful gulf has been
contaminated by greed. There's
a limit to the pleasures this world
will bestow.

EASY, MIDSHIPMAN

A slight indiscretion a long
time ago has caused us to grow
old. China's done away with shame
parades. Nothing you can do
in the house I can't do in the yard.
Domineering and overdressed, even
the Brahmin's dentist suffers
occasionally from bettor's elbow.
Colonel Corn will only communicate
in couplets starting tomorrow. Useless
as flashing a freight train. *Everything*
is already in the hands of the enemy.
Jimmy stole a motorcycle in Morocco,
and rode into Kew Gardens on the back
of a camel. We foraged for
raspberries and mixed them with
our ployes. Now we're drinking Moxie,
listening to Bach. This rural
hideaway is an acoustic powerhouse.
Will you be my hen of the woods?

JUNE YELLOWS IN JANUARY

We can't apply our will to nature
and not expect the same force brought
back down upon us. There's a law
written somewhere about that. Anchored
on terra firma, taken by the stars.
Trees that don't shed in winter are
said to stay awake through the night.
To keep a quiet vigil. Thawing is a
bottom up process. Quiet, continuous
energy at work underground. Picture
the buried stone, waiting all winter
for the warmth that will ferry it to the
surface. Easy to envision the Bacchanal
turning into a Vulcanal. Keep the pitch
from burning. The man of words is fascinated
by the man of action. Ironic that for dowsing
some have been burned at the stake. Of
all the Bachs, give me Edward. Newton
explained how the apple fell, but not how
it got up there in the first place.

CHATOOGA GARDENS

Our well-being is tied to the farmer's
good fortune. A green Christmas brings
a heavy harvest and a fat graveyard. One cloud
is enough to eclipse the sun. Clouds
that cast shadows also bring rain. Flame's
no longer welcome in the fire place; chimney
in need of restoration. Restore to these
woods their native spirit. Resist
that which resists in you. It's
hibiscus that causes the tea to resemble
blood. The religiously-muddled cling to
the notion they alone hold the keys to
the kingdom; this world is not their home
and they're content to destroy it. Let
the flute soothe your worried soul. Pan
plays a plaintive melody in the rowan
grove. Creatures of the sky wing their way
to hidden sanctuaries. The falcon doesn't
need to name the force that guides its flight.

AMPLE ENERGY AND SHINE

On the road to revelation, taking
liberties with the scriptures. What
direction are you counting from?
Take the tension out of your face;
no one's going to get hurt here.
Even a donkey is good for a laugh
or two. Pivot to the search. Punchy
and flexible, tipsy and dashing. His
dream is to live off wine and fish,
and never wear shoes again. Unlike
the maple leaves, I take my gloaming
first thing in the morning. Intensely
mellow hues. In one book you can
learn to rekindle the embers of love
and rid your village of scorpions. A
gift to the desirous, a luxury to the
seeker. When the sun's not busy
it ripens grapes.

GOOD GRIEF

The fruit is worthless but this
could be good rootstock. Would
that we could practice breeding
experiments on the aristocracy. Children
raised in high-ceilinged homes grow
up to be proud and tall. You
live in a turned-on world. Never ask
for what ought to be offered. Ask
the blind astronomer what it
means to rub oneself with chalk.
The light and shade of normal life.
My only ambition was to give
the bag a shake. Slip into indulgence.
Some see no mention of chopsticks or tea
as a sign Marco Polo never went to China.
Fundamentalists claim the world
is coming to an end, but fail to grasp
their culpability. The limit of vision
is not the limit of perception.

SWAN UPPING ON THE RIVER THAMES

Don't allow the golden Moses
to let you shirk the mountain stage.
A punchy climb. Ride the rare
lamprey to the super secret spot
that leaves even the locals shrugging.
What could this be but water? Throw
some Thursdays in there. The store-
front placard announced flameless
luminaries. Forced to attempt
impossible feats, then flogged when
they failed to flower. Off with his
thumbs. It's the most humane life-
altering punishment I can conjure.
Not a refinisher, a restorer. A leveling
wind. Over a week of en suite living
and I've finally bought a bar of soap.
Scoop some ice milk into the amberina
and regale us with tales of the Ice Glen.
The silly fiction of Priapus and the
Moon Bears. Oars up, grand seigneur.
Your cygnets have once again been weighed.

YOU NEVER SEE A DEAD VULTURE

Does the oak know when one
of its acorns takes root? Do
trees suffer survivors remorse?
Against your advisor's warnings
you set off for a night of passion
with your beloved, and are found
next morning at the bottom of
a cliff. It's not easy unpacking a
forest. As if to be standing in front
of a pear tree the moment buds
become visible. To see a different
mountain, a different martin. A
crack in your ice palace. Niveous;
snowy, or resembling snow.
Unsupported by bowman, you've
learned the danger of repenting.
Poached Eggs Esmeralda for the house!
The guy who spins the waltzers knows
every tune in 3/4 time.

A HOT STOVE IN SEASON

Tree just as tall underground. I grow
grain to feed savages. Something's
burning, but it doesn't smell malicious.
In exchange for your sweet
secretion I'll protect your soft body
between moltings. If you've ever had trouble
making snow break on the mountain,
the man with the melon holds the key
to good fortune. Attacked by a fit of
conscience, we'll be judged by what
we do on the ground. May you never
dawdle unwantonly. The music I listen to
in the mountains is not the music I listen to
when I long for the mountains. We've been watching
the wrong billiards game. You can see where
the monks once cut cabbages on this table.
You look very married; no wonder you talk to yourself.
You defend yourself with a weapon you cannot afford to use.

BARRAGE AT HAND

I realize my ideas will be discounted
because of my cynical cloak. I am not
one of Arcadia's lawless bandits.
Come bathe in my orchard or be catapulted
into an ornamental pond. Barefoot
without fear of moccasins. The heat
is more bearable if you don't have to move.
Clouds creep over the solarium. What
flavor of excitement are you in the mood for
today? Even diabetics can indulge
in the sugar-free rainbow stew. How
did this feeble god break his little finger?
What hill community was he charged to
protect? The shot seldom matches the
run. The first touch always lets you down.
The light of this hour reminds me
of cemeteries, serenity in the illusion
of eternity. All is temporal, geologically.
Rest in the immediate as though it were
infinity. You've sold the forest and
purchased trinkets in return. I hope
the birds don't blame us for their misfortune.

CONCEAL YOUR INTENT NO LONGER

It's all true and it's all false equally.
Perhaps it's the alignment of the stars
or that my food is slow. Nourishment
for the reflective mind, like fire conglobed
in highest cloud. Whet your appetite away,
but come home to eat. Commander Lee
is in the river with Mildred, washing their sins
away. Kicking Buddha's gong. I can't stand Scotch,
but love the sound it makes coming out
of the bottle. They're cloning Neanderthals
in northern Spain. This can only end in tears.
That's the second time tonight they've ended
with a seventh. A fidgety pick. Whatever
happened to the great empty spaces? Used
to be a man needed a gun to steal money.
My uncle calls the garbage dump our local
bird sanctuary. If you were a seagull I'd
call you King Oscar.

EARLY BIRD MOTIONS

Who are you to violate others
with your sense of understanding?
The reality shared by pen and page
is not that of the mouth and mind.
The forest is a place of hiding and of lurking.
The Perindens tree shelters doves
fleeing dragons. Faced with the looming
austerity, what supports your walk?
Dust off the chestnut. Point the telescope
at the nebulae. Retire into a
profound solitude. *Goodbye to the swift pony
and the hunt.* Coleridge read of Bartram's
travels through Georgia. Meditate on that
as you sit deep in the folds of the Land
of the Noonday Sun. Radical but not revolutionary,
a neutral agent. In search of the source of the misty ring.

EARLY EVERLASTING

Suspended in the mist, these
words like burrs in the mind. If
you don't freeze you may make it.
Some learn to build fires. Others
draw from the flame within.
Full of vim, a correct answer
will secure you a robe of honor and
a steed. What's more valuable, shade
every summer or warmth one winter
night? Gravestones covered with the
magnolia's large leaves. In each leaf
the design for its descent. Sing the song
of corrupted people as you stuff your
wallet with leaves. Only half-believe
what the mystics say. Born in the flames,
the pit will nurture you. The sea is on
top of the cottage. The notion there
are elements inside of us as old as the world.
The mysterious transition to enlightenment.
The Devyll is still a mechanism of the resistance.

SEASONAL HEATHEN

Don't wait until winter to learn
to weave. Negotiating reality
with your bees. Bees invented air
conditioning. This country hates
bankers, but commemorates the
demise of their tower with cries
and lamentations. Empty vessel.
Aroostook potatoes. All night toilet
paper. Had curried goat and went
for a walk on a beach. Three quarters
inch water five inches snow. What
about us is most prominent in the minds
of others? When you hear the tone you jump
into action. Sliced apple reconstitutes
dry tobacco. The right brushstroke.
Meerschaum (sea foam). The singing bone.
Some rocks get to live at Schoodic. Ignorant
of their meaning, we marvel at the warning sirens.

VARROA DESTRUCTOR

Too polite to be a nihilist,
he'll give you a bag of bees
and walk away. Three cheers
for the mound builders, the ray
that stung John Smith. Not just
cozy and obvious. We've
other trout to tickle. Tricked
into the desert sun. Everyone
has a door that must stay
shut. We've traveled back into
a new dark ages. If maggots
weren't inherent in the meat,
how did they get here? From the
venerable to the venereal. Young
and blithe, lithe in the finale. In the
midst of the madness it all made sense.

THE ARCHBISHOP OF ASTHMA

Sky gone all Rothko. Gather
into the owl's parliament and celebrate
your dividuality with what hovers and
what cowers. It isn't important to
address the trees with names imposed
on them by taxonomists. The trees
have a name for you different from the
one on your credit card. He's the kind
of man who'd give candy canes to raccoons,
then fill their tracks with corn meal.
Get the riddle size right. Rare as the grass
of Parnassus. Restrained with the acquisition
of wisdom. Find a stone to warm yourself on.
Impossible to gauge what sentience exists
in the space between water and steam. To
sense the meaningful response amid the noise.

OFF TO VILCAMBA

Let's plant the willow
that will be our legacy.
Which plant is the lynch-
pin? The discovery that
a plant could grow in a man-
made vessel. Not just
wither, the way the local god,
who sprang from this very
soil, did. Not every Pythia
is equally possessed. Your
answer will be ambiguous and
not always delivered in correct
hexameter. Learn to love
the infectious quiver. Gather
the restless, they that
would turn the world upside
down. Give a knock to
the skipper who can't find
a finish. No carvings to
suggest a purpose, big tress
but no shade. Defined by
your niche. Rely on the pro-
ducts of the chase. Long gone
looking for a new Sphinx, I've
become a stranger at home.

FEARLESS INSIDE THE FORTRESS

Soldier on without me; I've
lost my Cairn Terrier. A sprinkle
of salt will take the bite out of
Folgers. In man vs. sheep we're
armed to the hilt. Heaven knows
what fossil hunters will find here
next millennium. It's the last
hurrah at the petrol pump. The
brothel gives a discount to any
john on a bike. Amble up to the
speakeasy grille only to have Odin's
eye peeping back at you. Call me
Leafy Face, said the green man.
Dionysius retained the counsel of
Damon and Pythias. Jefferson isn't
acknowledged in Texas anymore. Ancient
variations play themselves out again.
A new dancer cribs an old chaconne.

ALL WITH BREAKING AS OUR END

Amputee athletes and the merits
of freezing as food preservation.
Front yard alive with robins, stoic
in the snow. Inclement weather brings
out breakfast fetishes. Nostradamus
even wrote a cookbook. You've
backed into the vision, but nothing's
broken. That's not blood, but
butterfly powder. We're all cosmopolitan
beside the wet bar. The hapless
pilgrims were rescued by Tony, the
former Futurist, and his intrepid
canine, Lotion.

SEASONS IN THE OPEN

Kiss me quick and candy
floss. The party will really
start when we get to Blackpool.
Born in a goatskin tent outside
the walls of Jericho, borne up
by strangers. This explains
your interest in heraldry. Impressive
meat locker. I admire your caveman
aesthetic, living pre-distillation.
If you have wind chimes, your neighbors
probably know it by now. Perhaps
it's my inclination towards monumentality,
but I can't give up wheat, staff of life.
What is it about the desert climate
that lends itself to excess? In his final
days he thought himself a kestrel.
There's no skeleton on Khufu's boat.

A WELTER OF CORMORANTS

If you're not too busy, my
house is on fire. No close-ups
please, I'm too old. Everything
can be mitigated with the proper
use of scented candles. The
Supreme Court turned the tomato
into a vegetable. Let's not tussle
on this sandy shore; share the shell.
Around here we say carapace.
You've a penchant for the superfluous.
Outfitting a bass boat with an
astrolabe. A moped with no petrol
is just a bike. Help yourself to as
many samosas as you think you
deserve, then go back for seconds.
If animals could talk there'd be
more vegetarians. The moon
shines enough light for the muskrats
to find their ramble. We found
a didgeridoo in Saskatchewan.
The most heavily-scored eleven
minutes of my life.

IN THE HAPPY BAG

I watched a miracle happen down
the street. I touched some vegetable
matter at the farmers market. Lost
in the lupine, it's hard to tell
how old this music is. The
winter agrimony sticks to your socks.
Follow swallows to the herbs that restore
eyesight. Florence Nightingale traveled
with an owl in her pocket. Music
itself seemed like a new invention. Four
years ago you couldn't pull a bird in
the disco. All he kept saying was,
Slovenia's shaped like a chicken.
Famous early in the morning, we mint
coins bearing a cephalophoric saint.

LAZARUS IN PROVENCE

The Judas fire is fueled on boxwood.
Saint Cornely protects the horned
animals. It is said Pilate refused
a basket of decorative eggs. How
does the Easter Bunny procure his
bounty? Confused by the arbitrary
arrangement of an alphabet inspired
by the flight formations of cranes.
I swear by the peacock my cactus
can count to twenty. I know my
succulents like an admiral knows
his ship. Bismarck hugged a tree to
recover from fatigue. I place my faith
in the hazelnut. Just because it's found
in a tree doesn't make honey a fruit.
Pliny thought honey was the saliva of
stars. The honey you stole from the bees
will soothe the wounds inflicted in the process.

THE ULTIMATE CREEPER

Buttermilk sky and a tinny cornet
coming from across the hedgerow. The
shy neighbor keeps a menagerie in his
potting shed. If it's a living thing with
teeth, it probably bites. I burned
you to make you stronger. Far be it
from me to press a friend to the mat.
The worst way to lose weight is through
worry. Who would go back to Antarctica
just to fetch Falcon Scott's frozen sack
of butter? Parts of Pompeii still smell
of garum. The Israelites looked back
with longing at the garlic fields of Egypt.
I always come back with a witty quip
an hour after I've been insulted. Take
the hammer to the tenth. What're you
going to do with that last rock? Whig
out the naïve angler with the gar's green bones.

FLORIDA WATER

Free to roam, but just
as soon settle down. The
system is under pressure, though
what with these faultless skies
you'd never know. Always wanting
to replicate good results, we
throw out ill omens just because.
I don't want to see the smoke
from another man's chimney or hear
the sound of another man's axe. After
noon before the sun finds our little
spot on happy hill. A land
unmarred by the engines of war.
Do you know the moment is perfect
when you're in it, or does that
realization come with reflection? Hawk
circles in the azure, above the
canopy of trees. Below, a leaf
lands on stone, scattering Juncos.

STRANGERS TAKE IT AWAY

A fine piece of hitting makes
the closer put his lid back on.
Colors I haven't conjured in years
come to me from out of the blue.
I can't tell how it's called, but I can
tell its history. It was back when
everybody was big into colloidal
silver. My sister got married &
left me her flute. Picture two men
locked in a room who've separately
been told they're the other man's
executioner. Watch what's visible
of the tree's movement. The reason
will come later. Swift passage,
unbending vision. The moon activates
the owls & agitates the waters.
Honor the number you're given,
remember the victims of shipwreck
& lighthouse fire. Riding a caleche
drawn by a single steed, the positive
trend may be temporary. Riding a
hobby horse into the Guadalupe
Mountains, the beginning of the roar
comes from somewhere not the throat.

FRESHWATER EVIDENCE

Drawer too full of pistols to find a fresh
bookmark. Marking my page in Barrett's
Magus with a takeout flyer from Guadalupana,
whose beef tongue burritos I adore. If I lived on an
ait in the Narraguagus I could watch eagles feeding
on both banks. Whenever I come to call you're
either combing your hair or drying wheat. Would
that I could make the music that comforts me.
Still not sure what the neutrino offers. As near
to nothing as we know. Never alone in sunlight.
Sun as horse, as the nag is said to whinny.
The fiery backbone, the first body fossil we've found.
Shooting too heavy to come from thugs, silences
pregnant with further meaning. Funerals for the
protestors further inflaming the unrest. Taboos are
of no use to us. Remember the sacrifices that took
place on that hill, just before the motorway.

BALM AGAINST ALL MELANCHOLY

Stout yeoman, softnecked pioneer,
there's no road along which we can
further go. The technology escapes
me, but there must exist a means
by which we can keep the cabin illumined.
The past is gone; the future knocks
but once. Those intent upon conquest
should study the hapless merganser in
the midst of the fox. Agile cutpurses
move about like butter in the pan. Sugary
talk of trefoils and butterflies gives
way to hypodermic needles and prophylactics.
Juniper berries for the waxwings; the
number of berries foretells the severity
of winter. Good looks wear thin before
the sun comes up. Young druids leap
forth and test the elk.

VERBUM CORDIS

It was a slog just getting
to Ushant. Following the soft
edge, repairing in the glisses.
This is the only place a man can cop
to being a screwup and receive
a round of applause. Read on
to learn why pregnant women
should avoid Maori artifacts.
The Salamis Stone may help you
measure the Parthenon, but it
does nothing to explain Dan Patch's
pace mile. The candle only smells
sweet after the burning. To be the
family terrified by a cylindrical cloud.
The boiling fog. We don't all start
from a pure zero. If I knew where
the vitality dwelt I'd direct more
nourishment there.

WHEN SULEIMAN TAKES ROME

Sweat of the sun, tears
of the moon. Experiment
with the listening, rejoice
in natural forms. There are
things happening on the page
I can't account for in the reading.
Is anything broken
here? Certainly the week's strongest
empire. Another finger's
floated down river tied to a log.
Bede can tell you how to count to
a million on your fingers. Don't
rely on Dürer for an accurate
rhinoceros. It's impossible
to reckon a true year without the
concept of the fraction. It's beyond
the ken of these symbols to share
the whole reality I envision.
I always seem to be one word off
from the one in my head. Unfamiliar echo.
My garden is overrun but not with weeds.

STAG PARTY

Rescued from the open ocean
only to drown in the motel jacuzzi.
Mauler on the edge, what shape
will your vengeance take? Dial up
an exotic pressure; I'm all a-
tingle, anticipating the showdown.
Defender on his hip, the sheriff
conducts a swift machine. A tumbrel
with a vanity plate. A brisk parade
from the market to the bunker and
my body breaks into tears. It's never
hot at the right time. Nice beefsteak,
Soapy. If you don't have tongs use
your fingers. Squeeze the bereaved's
arm, there's elbow-bending in the backroom.

FEAST OF HEALING

Until the osprey tears it
from the water, the fish only knows
a liquid dimension. You cannot solve
a problem with the same mind that
created it. A dolphin is more than
a fish which changes its colors when dying.
I am not a fisherman, I am a man of the sea.
Birds get to wear feathers because they figured
out how to fly. We can't fly, but we can dance
like cranes. If Brigid were here we'd only
have to kill one chicken. Carve an idol
from tallow. Place it on the hearthstone
and watch it melt away. In the Pythagorean
view of things, look for a heron in the next go
around. We're all cut from the same bolt of light.
Our energy creates powerful winds. If you live in
dry country, this poem will bring you rain.

EVER FUGITIVE (ANOTHER ALCHEMICAL POEM)

If we were to look at reality
unaided by the filter of perception
we would be blinded. To see
the fire inside green wood. To
catch dragonflies, appeal to their
desire to rise above their peers.
The sound of song birds, attractively
measurable. No wind to shiver in.
A warmth somewhere between the
human body and June sunshine.
No one knows when the last weariness
will come. Hannibal marched his elephants
past innumerable Burma Shave signs. A poor
finish for a man of his standing. Poison
in the ring. We have the measurement but
not the time. Five is a fortuitous number.
Five stones from which man first extracted
copper. Melanosis is the first stage
towards transmutation. Teach your
acolyte a few illusions and let him loose
upon the world.

PARENT FLAME

Came too late to catch my azalea. Blue
Jays hop among Cheddar Pinks. What are
the bigger themes? Pattern of contamination,
scale of release. Get the right ship in place;
we'll weep when the crisis's over. Kiss the
wizard, catch a magical bug. Working through
a bout of serenity, everything's more complicated.
Even silence. Impossible to contact the feelings
in others. There's nothing beyond the fireworks.
The couscous is bigger twenty miles away. The
men who walked on the moon are now quite
elderly. Keep rodents off Nightingale. Go
into the forest to achieve liberation. You have
more freedom than you use. Glint when sun-
light hits your beard. *Like two dogs that do
not hurt our limbs.* Metallurgy at home ends
with an ugly bit of cauliflower in your furnace.
The wandering mendicant has no memory of
ever being illiterate.

MOONSEEDS

AFTERNOON THEATRE

Let me step out of the picture.
Calibrate the happiness. A tincture
of thorn apple and you'll be the
next Turner. Take the calcium
ferry to the toy farm; the winter
traveler looks to bed in skunk
cabbage. Into the undulations.
There's a windmill in France that's
been spinning since 1555. Don't
throw all your energy into one wind.
Spoil the sprinter's rhythm. Running
out of favors. *The poor live in the bushes.*
The claustrophobia has a point. Like the songs
we sang together in the shelter. Listening
to a Dane conveying the sounds of
the middle east. Music to be eaten
alive by. Eating a bowl of Hungarian cowboy
soup. Rough and honest, humble and oily.
Those who call for war should not be responsible
for growing our food. Searching for sustenance,
only offered rhetoric. No space at Nature's table.

BLIZZARD OF INTRUDERS

I'll probably end my days
in a cave, ironing cabbage leaves,
living for the weak end. Dying
of an abscessed tooth. As empires
grow so do epidemics. Grow
or don't grow. Conquered but given
geese as consolation. *Geese*
lower their heads in order to pass
under a bridge, no matter how
high its arches are. From huts
and granaries to the Cosmati
Pavement. Flowers like the open
mouths of barking dogs. We
gave leprosy to armadillos, and
now they're giving it back. A
marmot in central Asia nearly
killed us all. Families of the violently-
killed are outraged by history's objectivity.
Rip the pretentious. A person born
on the plains will conceive a treeless Eden.

INVOCATION OF SIX HEAVENS

Such looking as we have done from
this vista. Coast of light. Provinces
like twigs outside the web's reach.
Thwarted child sacrifice on Beal's
Island. Chased a tickle across the
border. The Dutchman's strong legs.
Power he knows how to generate. Ride
with suppleness, ripen the aniseed.
Imaginary dryness, heavy calamity.
The bag lacks flour. *That we will*
sleep at evening, and be free for ever.
What did the Minoans call themselves?
Did the Callatians really consume
their father's corpses? Forsake the
cave, those things you've not made
peace with. The crickets are inter-
changeable. Enduring and anonymous.
Among the ten thousand. White horse
in fog, lost on the cobblestones. Night
watchman of Lausanne, at work from
ten to two. Would all this travel have
been worth it if one day we could sit in
a room and have images of idyllic land-
scapes projected onto a screen in front
of us? *We walked for three months in*
the forest. Crossed North Potato Creek

in Copper Basin, the Continental Divide
at Cowee Gap. Bear holes in the unknown
crop. First used to pack porcelain, now
invasive on the east coast. *They come
from the north and use magic.* To be in
a misty forest and feel the spirits moving.
To sustain the uncontainable expression.
Thunder before the sun. More noise
than the leaves can buffer.

LIVING WITHOUT MIRRORS

All the texts that shaped our thinking
have been disproved. Did the king ever
really have to stand on one foot? What
will restore our serenity? *It is vain*
to comfort the grieving for grief must have
its fill. We never used to see raptors
above the city. Invasion of sanctuary.
Open season on proselytizers. As one century
struggled to reconcile geology's revelations,
we wrestle with astrophysics. From terra
firma to the extra terrestrial. When the
lights first went on in the universe. The multi-
verse. The energy that holds everything
together. The detritus of yesterday's dis-
order is offered to the creator of ruins. *Some*
will burn with fire, applied, it may be,
to punish, or it may be to heal. One day we
will sit in the shade of the trees we have planted.

MARSH MARIGOLD, YOU ARE MY DIVINITY

More choices means more discontentment.
The faster the pea spins, the slower
its clock gets. In between Mahler and
the crows, from here to the sunshine.
Turning the caged staff with the left hand.
Driven mad by narcissus, a somber tempest.
A dry moat filled with thistles. Wrangle the
sound, the flow of swords forward. An arc,
an anchor. The resurrected animal.
Balanced and complicated. Wild bounce
of the drunken, fragmented mind. Mozart
is hard. Suss it out. Harmonic language.
At any moment, what you hear is what
you hear. Shadow the word. The haze.
He gets it right like that. He knows what
people not to feel sorry for himself in front
of. Intermezzo. Xerxes and his plane mistress.
To dye one's hair with saffron and drink
date palm wine from a unicorn's horn.
It's fear that's left the monument untouched.
The mountain, whose spirit possesses the dancers.

PILGRIM'S CHOICE

First you need an Ethiopian
scale. Just as the geranium
needs the bee's buzz. Sounds
bounce around this contemporary baffle-
ment. The unmoved mover *continually*
shapes the world with a purpose.
Radical even in a time of ferment.
Eat the fruit and let others misconstrue
the meaning. Gather rose hips to stave
off scurvy. Gather ye oak galls
while ye may. Who was it
who thought the written word would
be the death of memory? Compose
a list of deadly inhalants. As
the freeway goes the way of the
Roman road, so the rose has
lost its scent. Gilded with
bruises. Cleansed with fire. Hosed
down by King Neptune's disturbance
regime. Heretic is a title conferred.
Kindly stand out of my sunlight.

THE ARTIFICIAL SOMNAMBULIST

Funny how revolution quells one's
interest in mesmerism, the maintenance
of humanity, the metals needed for life.
Sheltered from the killing winds. Hotter
shades nearer the house. How does
this compare to what's hanging on the
ropes? *In this corner of life I look for self-*
realization. Red sails at sunset. *What*
you lose on the swings you gain on the
roundabouts. Living in the shadow side
of freedom. No uniform current. To see
the sun without fear. The eyes to brighten.
The music makes you naked. The leaves
you touch with your feet, gold and vigorous.
Ash tree, tree of life. Cassia, tree of life. Fig
tree, tree of heaven. Oak tree, tree of life.
Sycamore, tree of life. Cypress, tree of eternal
death. *In truth it is the worst of human ills, to*
abound in knowledge and yet have no power
over action. The king soaped his head and dis-
tributed gifts. I took from what was on the page.

THE HERMIT'S HOURGLASS

Now I love covered wagons
as much as the next guy. Common
corn flag, important as the poles.
Blurred and shifting, bowing
on the edges. Trapped in hardship,
sustained by the divine yolk. Easy
to forget the cicadas, quiet underground
this year. When the experiments
aren't going well, astonish the homefolks
with a smuggled chameleon. Sleepy,
slow and sweeping, the stubborn searcher
must look inside to see the winds.
Dowse for malachite until the signals
are certain. Like a duck with talons,
a little beast the size of a chicken. Throwing
out chicken feed, hoping to grow poultry.
Don't let La Tunda fart on the shrimp. Agrippa's
dog was not the devil. Murderers
in this life become house cats in the next.
Stealthy as the velvet worm. By nibbling
your toes I can tell if you're a virgin. *No*
need to wear a toga, the neighbors
do not come to call.

VALLEY SANCTUARY

Paralyzed by fears at night that
don't even register during day. Defending
the border of a hostile imagination.
Where are the wondrous animals that
will unlock the misery we're living in?
Attend to various pleasures, populate
the vibrations. Learn to sing with your
mouth closed. Golden chime. A fishing
tabernacle floored in stumps and knuckle
bones. A tenuous connection with
the outside world, trying to arrange
a binding. The crystal has grown
dark. The dove, country pigeon, bobs
and scurries with its mate. It
rains, it snows, where's the tomato?
How fast can you row away from a
former friend you once shared Xmas
dinner with? Panic down by the water.
Cleanse the wristwatches, the wandering
uterus of Beirut. There've been no
good statues since the invention of trousers.
Of leaving, of arriving. I don't drink
but have been known to sniff dough. As
the baker manages his yeasts, no un-
believer was allowed to eat oranges in
Moorish Spain. How many had to be stricken

before a plant's poisonous nature was common
knowledge? To live, to die, healed.

VILLEGGIATURA

Let's assign new names to the meadow
grasses, now that we've studied their natures
in each hour of light. A hint of the
weather, scents of lavender and rue. Like
Icarus on a cloudy day. A stillness that
gives butterflies precision. *But so very*
few know of the aloneness, the trial,
the battles fought on the plane of the
imagination, the fear, the visitation of
the god. Relearning to work the mirror,
ceremony of the moment. From Aaron's
rod to the magician's wand. Can your
staff produce almonds? Coconuts are good
for the bones. He's a stoner but he knows
his birds. The horse sprung from Poseidon's
trident, Norsemen from an ash tree. Never mind
horses can't sit down, moonwort will unshoe
them. Woe to those who'd throw monkshood
in a well. Misery not surrogate, a lyric
pulled from the visual. As three to eleven,
so the moon to the mile.

CATHEDRAL RING

TEST MILE

Lost the big herbivores but gained
all these trees. *The fir tree is formed*
like a flame and is thus the Universal
Root, the foundation of all things.
Enormous and immediate, the dynamic
expression. Alive in a molecular world.
A world estranged from the Mysteries,
reduced to fingering detective fiction.
Science is great when it confounds
fundamentalists, not when it modifies
corn. In the front room pounding
Beethoven with the door locked. Sleeping
with too many afghans. Staff around
to make life nicer. Knit me a corgi.
I was thinking about it and then I was there.
Not important what others call it, so long
as you have a name for it. As the
monarch follows the milkweed. The king
in the custard pie. Even his bookmarks
are interesting. The temptation to be smart.
To dwell inside a cave and glow green
from living off nettles. We are the mountain.

STORMSVALA

Step back in time and pick up
the notch. Pinch a cutting from
the plant that sets you on fire.
We had peacocks and now we have
coffeepots. Xenophon hunted ostriches
on the banks of the Euphrates. Lot
of horse in Portland. *Why don't we
send her off to the breeding shed and
let her be a mom?* Everyone has side-
burns, no one has a phone. They
won't let you put in at Patriot Lake.
This is my boat and I'll push it myself.
At home with his vessel. Sailing on
top of deep waters, old china and bones
fathoms below. A diplomatic response
to the showboating. There's no good
time to be made a vassal. The egalitarian
view the rich should order the poor about
with kindness. The dumpy herdsman
caught longing for smallpox, killed by
hail in summer.

THUNDER EGG

Birds all dart and chortle. Open space
so full of animal sex. Curvy tree no
hiding in wind. Tent alabaster in composure,
a hiding in there. Squirrel no knot in bark,
much less two. Mistaking the shaking maple
for a sprinter. Light the blue touchpaper and
the candy cannon says pop. Garden party just
beyond the Himalayan rhubarb. Hungry enough
to eat a hosta. What did the Romans call Good
King Henry? *I have eaten two humans—one was*
a man, the other a woman … They taste the same.
Not saying much, being legal in a country that
stole its land from the natives. Let's go where
the ignorance is more novel. Hail, valiant traveler.
It's Wonderland or Bust. Wandering on the mall,
chewing on a puffin. When the band turns up,
it's all getting started.

TYPO NEGATIVE

How did they measure hail before golf
balls? Rain comes down all that heavy,
filling the peacepool. *Let but a little*
cloud appear when I have found the river
that is to help us. All of a sudden
a lot of periscopes. Bathe the ambrosial
stone, underneath the word Wednesday. How
can you talk with the door open?
At the market without a basket, the sign
said she had risen. Hard to be informal
with a sword. Delight on the balcony. Re-
introduce pattern where it went missing.
Compose it as it happens. If the tornado
wants the windows open, it'll open them.
I'm not convinced by you caduceus. I
don't trust my emotions after noon. *I*
used to ride a fast pig, and was so happy
when it turned into bacon. The nourishing reward.

STONE ROLLER

Trade paint deep in the stretch.
A dream of a swan in a bear trap.
Squeaky on tiptoe, red cherry on
top of the mountain. Mulberries
and medlars. Ask the Perfect
Serpent, we've never known it
so dear. I wonder what Sitting
Bull thought, reenacting Little
Bighorn, for paying crowds, in
Buffalo Bill's Wild West Show?
Blind Dunnock, can't you see
the Cuckoo laid an egg in your nest?
Living as a hunchback, geese foraging
for pulses. Simple turtle, uncooperative
mice. Making up words to The Hussite
Song. Rest easy, rendering you into oil
is no longer feasible. His is a voice that
carries, but not much.

PERSONAL SYNTHESIS

Take off your cap and stick out
your tongue, oh wise one. *Learn*
to know all, but keep thyself unknown.
Who made fire to shine? What's
the protocol for washing these old
fashioned pigs, poor-sighted quadrupeds?
It's not like working in the city,
mending pipes. Miolnir was Thor's
hammer. We're on the ground less than
a thousand months. That wasn't me,
but my grandfather, who used to hop
on your resting face. It's not how you move
but what moves you. Maybe it wasn't cheap,
the coping stone. The questionable pocket.
An old story in a new language. Either
a lodge in the distance or a pilgrim's water
bottle. Leave the spoon in the bowl.

HOLOCENE TO ANTHROPOCENE

We identify with the popular
image of the post-apocalyptic
survivor, yet can't see ourselves
as part of the initial mass
die-off. We want to be around
for the bitter end. Ask the creatures
of chalk about Time's hierarchy.
What time I am afraid I will trust
in trees. The cloud forest, the sacred
grove. The space where words wait
to be invented. Tempting conjecture,
dances in dark blue and ivory. Ideas
so dangerous they can only be expressed
in the wild. An insight not yet vulgar.
What do the birds of Dodona tell us
today? Lost in a book of mazes, a
mock eruption gives shape to your
incoherent vision. We grow out of
our gills in the womb. Hesiod
believed our age would end when
babies were born white-haired. The
white wolf sits again on a branch outside
the window.

(GONE) TO THE FIELDS OF ASPHODEL

The moment Giacomo says he feels
the sun, we start. Are the people
going to get haircuts? Will the ostrich
rear its head? The woodland outside
the walled garden is full of fox, their
strange ways. Creeping yellow feet, color
of power. Desperate to achieve surprise.
The falling star is heavier than I am.
The bite in the pepper; jangle of bananas,
they smell like what they are. Tearing
noise of roots. Venus Looking Glass
dies immediately upon cutting. *When*
you see a babushka selling vegetables,
you know they didn't come from Spain.
Personal charm and powerful links are
no match for the new viruses. Obelisk
behind the car park reminds us cultures
are impermanent. Reptiles had their
dominance. It takes a lot of blood
to circle the pond.

BOW STREET RUNNERS

Keep a weathered eye out. Even old ducks
like a bit of smut. Twenty four minutes
into Arthur, wind on the leading edge. Various
air movements in multiple layers of the
atmosphere. Ice crystals cause the lightning.
Inside the proportions trees grow in. I don't
know what's wrong, but I know what makes
me angry. Make a fist, don't laugh. You'll
give up eventually. The words for dolphin *delphis*
and womb are similar in the Greek. Swear *delphus*
upon the bristly boar, titular spiv. The snail
men, whose silvery trail is wisdom. The
miraculous trout of Sligo. Lost the heat, but
still lots of instability. A calm night so far.
Easy to live here when everyone's out of town.
When this passes, we're done.

A FULL DAY WORTH OF CHANGING

If you start handing out
money, we'll never get out
of here. Sitting on blue
Morocco, you've developed a
drug-resistant melancholy. The
black bile of dejection. Reject
the yellow carnation. The artificial
word. Why would there be
pageantry at 6AM? The rod of office carries
instant sophistication; crack and glow.
In the foot of Island Forty,
what appears as a rainbow is actually a flaming
bridge. Fiberglass Aphrodite. A bamboo cricket
called Conscience. A bowl of mercury.
Standing waves in the emulsion. Fabulous
adjustment within the archery of the system.
Neatest thing since the lateen sail.

FOREMOST OF THE WESTERNERS

Remember what hand position to
use next time you're attacked by
an elephant. The older I get the
less I care about pretending to know
everything. You got the right answer
but asked the wrong question. The train
sounds closer than usual, but the
tracks've not been moved. A voyage
would accomplish nothing. Sixty years
of flea powder for your pet giraffe.
Tapwater turned flammable by fracking
turns the locals rowdy. Let's turn
these coal mines into cheese caves.
Black birds shaped like cartoon cigars.
Youthful exuberance amid volcanic
ash. Imagine a pushy dame name Annabel,
unsympathetic to children, splitting poly-
anthus. Come in when you hear the chainsaw.
A garden with good bones. Those who think
dinosaur bones are a hoax. A conjuring act
with a long shelf life. At the Last Judgment,
Osiris will be chagrinned so few people know
who he is.

www.ingramcontent.com/pod-product-compliance
Lightning Source LLC
Chambersburg PA
CBHW020938090426
42736CB00010B/1187